MULTIPLE MEANINGS
IN AMERICAN
SIGN LANGUAGE

Brenda E. Cartwright and Suellen J. Bahleda

RID Press
Registry of Interpreters for the Deaf
333 Commerce St, Alexandria, VA 22314
703.838.0030 (V), 703.838.0454 (FAX), 703.838.0459 (TTY)
www.rid.org

Registry of Interpreters for the Deaf

RID is a national membership organization representing the professionals who facilitate communication between people who are deaf or hard of hearing and people who can hear. Established in 1964 and incorporated in 1974, RID is a tax-exempt 501(c)(3) nonprofit organization.

It is the mission of RID to provide international, national, regional, state and local forums and an organizational structure for the continued growth and development of the profession of interpretation and transliteration of American Sign Language and English.

RID Press is the professional publishing arm of RID. The mission of RID Press is to extend the reach and reputation of RID through the publication of scholarly, practical, artistic and educational materials that advance the learning and knowledge of the profession of interpreting. The Press seeks to reflect the mission of RID by publishing a wide range of works that promote recognition and respect for the language and culture of deaf people and the practitioners in the field.

RID Press is a division of the Registry of Interpreters for the Deaf, 333 Commerce St, Alexandria, VA 22314, USA, (703) 838-0030, (703) 838-0459 TTY, www.rid.org

Published 2009

Library of Congress Control Number: 2009927114

ISBN 978-0-916883-51-5

Printed in the United States of America

Contents

Authors' Note

Our goal in creating this book is to provide a tool that assists learners across the whole continuum of American Sign Language (ASL) proficiency to approach English vocabulary conceptually so they can produce more precise equivalent meanings in ASL. The process of developing this book has energized and challenged us to evaluate and rethink our own instructional approaches and materials. We believe this book captures that energy and will support and enhance the creation of equivalent meanings in expressive signing and interpreting for a variety of learners: ASL students, developing interpreters in training programs, as well as working interpreters. We greatly appreciate and wish to express our gratitude to the students, workshop participants and esteemed colleagues who served as our testing ground and provided many invaluable suggestions in the development of this book.

Brenda E. Cartwright, M.S.
CSC, CI and CT
Bcartwright@lcc.edu

Suellen J. Bahleda, M.Ed., M.DIV
CI and CT
rwpress@juno.com

Preface

There are a variety of ways one can use this book to improve one's signing and interpreting skills. Teachers and students may choose to explore one particular unit or a variety of elements from different units. This book assists in developing and practicing a process for analyzing the meaning of specific English words and phrases so that one can create accurate equivalents in ASL. It is crucial that learners avoid the temptation to hurry through any exercise, even when a word or phrase seems easy or obvious. By taking the time to analyze and determine the meanings of the various words and phrases in the exercises within this book, a process for analyzing meaning emerges which serves as a foundation for analyzing the meaning of English words and phrases and translating this meaning accurately, efficiently and proficiently into ASL.

Introduction

The English language is complex, containing an extensive variety of vocabulary as a result of its rich linguistic history. While this is one of its strengths, it is also one of its greatest challenges for persons translating or interpreting content from English into another language. Because English contains an extensive number of words with multiple meanings and functions, as well as an abundance of idiomatic phrases, creating accurate translations to and from other languages is a dynamic, thought- and message-driven process - not a simple one driven by individual words viewed in isolation.

English is most commonly the native language of American Sign Language (ASL) students and interpreters, and the complexities of English are often not given much thought until one attempts to translate a message into another language. Most native users of English are adept at using an extensive array of words and phrases to express a variety of meanings. This can be a wonderful asset in translating and interpreting between English and ASL. However, the challenge occurs in attempting to find just the precise sign or phrase in ASL that expresses a specific meaning expressed in English. Creating accurate translations and interpretations of English into ASL requires more than simply learning a body of signed vocabulary that match English words.

ASL is also a rich and complex language, expressed visually-manually. As such, it uses linguistic elements that differ from an aural-oral language such as English. These include space, a spectrum of visual description elements, facial expression and body movement—elements that can be layered because they can occur simultaneously. Learning to incorporate ASL linguistic elements such as these, in addition to using accurate ASL vocabulary, is the key to producing the exact meaning that one intends. The goal of this book is to aid students in experimenting with using ASL to express a multitude of meanings from English.

Unit One:

One Word, Many Meanings

To convey the meaning of a message in one language into another, a process of analysis must take place. The specific meaning of the source language must be determined. Words themselves do not occur in isolation: even the word "stop" on a sign is accompanied by a particular color and shape of the sign to convey information about its specific meaning.

The meaning of a word (or group of words) is determined by taking into account the context in which it occurs. Studying particular English words across a range of contexts can improve one's ability to quickly determine the specific meaning of certain English words. The meaning of an English word and how it functions in a particular context must be analyzed in order to produce its equivalent in ASL. An ASL equivalent may be produced using a single sign that has a one-to-one, word-to-sign correspondence or may require several signs to convey the meaning from English into ASL.

Analyzing for Meaning

There are many words in English that change in meaning, depending upon how they are used in different contexts. For example, the word "fall" can be used in various ways to mean different things. A variety of those meanings can be seen in the following sentences:

1. Don't run around the pool, you might fall!
2. The leaves turn such beautiful colors in the fall.
3. Gibbon wrote *The Decline and Fall of the Roman Empire.*
4. Some people fall in love on their first date.
5. You know what they say about Charlie: the apple doesn't fall far from the tree.

Since "fall" has a different purpose and meaning in each of these English sentences, it would be signed differently for each sentence, to reflect the various uses. To determine the ASL equivalent or accurate translation for each use of the word "fall," it is essential to go through a process of analysis for each sentence/context.

The first step in the process of analysis used in determining an ASL equivalent is to decide whether the meaning of an English word is represented by the single word or functions as part of a (larger) phrase. In the sample sentences above, the meaning of the word "fall" is represented by the single word "fall" in sentences #1-3 but functions as part of a phrase in #4-5. When a word functions as part of a phrase, the phrase must be analyzed for meaning as a whole, rather than determining the meanings of the individual words as they might be used in isolation.

The next step in the analysis process is to think more deeply about what the word or phrase actually means. As part of the analysis process, consider how it might be defined in a dictionary or how the meaning might be described or explained to a person who had never before seen or heard that word or phrase.

In sentence #1, a standard or literal definition is used for "fall;" the meaning being to lose one's footing and drop suddenly and involuntarily. There is an equivalent single ASL sign to express this meaning of that word. Part of the richness and complexity of ASL, however, allows this sign, which has a one-to-one, word-to-sign correspondence, to be modified to show the nature of the fall; a stumble, a full fall forward or backward, and the landing.

The word "fall" in sentence #2 also has a literal definition meaning the season of the year, also known as "autumn." Again, there is a one-sign equivalent in ASL to express this meaning of the word. This sign is different from the one used to express the meaning in sentence #1 because the meaning being expressed is different.

In sentence #3, "fall" is used as part of a title. Proper names, titles, etc. are fingerspelled, even when there are possible sign equivalents. Another example, "Blue's Clues," would be fingerspelled, even though there is an ASL equivalent for the word "blue."

Sentence #4 uses "fall" within an English idiomatic phrase. There is a one-sign ASL equivalent for the phrase, although most English idioms do not have a one-sign equivalent. As with the first example in sentence #1, facial expression and body movement can be used to accompany this ASL sign to indicate the intensity of the "fall."

Sentence #5 also involves an English idiomatic phrase; however, in this case, there is not a one-sign equivalent in ASL that expresses the meaning of this idiom. One needs first to consider what meaning is intended by the use of this phrase - the precise meaning that is being expressed in English. Once that has been determined, it is possible to create a sign phrase that will convey an equivalent meaning in ASL.

Analyzing for Function

In the analysis process, it is important to remember that English words can serve a number of linguistic functions. The way a word operates is an important aspect of the analysis process when creating translation matches or equivalents. Consider how the word "milk" functions in the following sentences:

1. Harvey Milk lived in San Francisco.
2. Please bring home a gallon of milk.
3. Ernie went out to milk the cows.
4. Siobhan has milky white skin.
5. Don't cry over spilt milk.

"Milk" is used here as a proper name, a noun, a verb, an adjective and within an idiomatic phrase. To create an equivalent in ASL, it is important to consider both meaning <u>and</u> function.

In sentence #1, "milk" is used as a proper name and thus would be fingerspelled.

In sentence #2, "milk" is used as a noun and has a one-sign equivalent in ASL.

In sentence #3, "milk" is used as a verb. An ASL equivalent must show the action, whether Ernie is milking cows by hand or using a milking machine.

Sentence #4 uses a variant on the word "milk" as an adjective. Conveying the idea of "milky white skin" is a descriptive process in ASL. There are qualities about this person's skin, other than the color, that make it "milky," which need to be expressed in ASL, perhaps by describing smoothness, purity, lack of blemishes, etc.

"Milk" is used within an idiomatic phrase in sentence #5. Deciding what is meant by the idiomatic phrase as a whole determines the ASL phrase that would convey an equivalent meaning.

The exercises in this book will provide practice in analyzing English words with multiple meanings and some English idioms for their meaning and function across a spectrum of uses. Some uses may seem easier to translate or interpret than others, but do not be tempted to cut short the analysis process and jump to quickly choosing sign equivalents. Practicing the analysis process with a variety of examples will build a foundation that can be applied to the wide spectrum of English words with multiple meanings that one may encounter when translating, interpreting or otherwise engaging in clearly signing one's meaning in ASL.

Group One: A Rainbow of Meanings

Consider how the target word is used in each sentence. Examine its context, analyzing for meaning and function. Explore potential sign or sign-string translations for the target word. Sign each sentence in ASL, choosing the translation that reflects the meaning as accurately as possible.

BLUE
The sky is blue.
Li felt a little blue yesterday.
Jay likes to listen to the blues.
Frank received a job offer out of the blue.
Edward Fairfax Rochester was a blue blood.
I checked the "Blue Book" to see how much I could get for my 1968 Pontiac GTO.

GREEN

My son bought a green car.

Aunt Della used dandelion greens in the salad.

Larry was green with envy when Maggie got the promotion.

The pears were too green to eat.

Tiger's chip-shot landed on the green.

RED

The flag is red, white and blue.

Kari doesn't eat red meat.

The thief was caught red-handed.

Sean needs help cutting through the red tape for his application for benefits.

The battleship went on red alert.

Let's paint the town red tonight!

YELLOW

The Yellow Sea divides China and the Korean Peninsula.

Diana prefers yellow roses.

Wesley wouldn't take the dare because he was yellow.

To lower your cholesterol, don't eat the egg yellow.

Don't eat yellow snow!

WHITE

Beat the egg whites to make a fluffy meringue.

I'm dreaming of a white Christmas.

Melvin wears white socks and sandals, no matter what the season.

There's a new security fence around the White House.

Don't shoot until you see the whites of their eyes!

Franklin has a white collar job.

My third grade teacher was Mrs. White.

Group Two: Meanings From Head to Toe

EAR

The science class made a model of an ear.

Ella ate three ears of corn at supper.

Mike's mom told him to clean his room, but it went in one ear and out the other.

When the conversation turned to gossip, Margo was all ears.

Friends! Romans! Countrymen! Lend me your ear!

Alberto has a tin ear.

EYE

Bill has brown eyes.

The eye of the needle was too small for the thread.

The cameraman was stuck in the eye of the hurricane.

The stray dog eyed the bones in the butcher shop window.

We planted the potato eyes.

NOSE

The clown has a red nose.

The nose of the airplane was painted green.

Liz's guess of 5,721 jellybeans in the jar was right on the nose.

Jan always sticks her nose where it doesn't belong.

Rising gas prices mean consumers pay through the nose at the pumps.

The favorite horse won the Belmont Stakes by a nose.

FINGER

Henry has very long fingers.

The children's menu included spaghetti, hot dogs and chicken fingers.

Mugsy fingered the ringleader for the cops.

The party snacks were all finger foods.

The motel beds each came with a Magic Fingers machine.

THUMB

The teacher had the class under her thumb.

I will thumb a ride to Portland, OR.

Katrina has a green thumb.

I am all thumbs when it comes to car repair.

Humans have an opposable thumb.

Whitley tends to thumb her nose at the rules.

SHOULDER

Padded shoulders go in and out of fashion.

When the car's radiator overheated, we pulled over onto the shoulder.

Parents must shoulder the responsibility for their children's behavior.

John shouldered his backpack for the 25-mile hike.

Sandra just needed a shoulder to cry on for a while.

I got a pass to an Oscar party and got to rub shoulders with all the celebrities!

TONGUE

Danny stuck his tongue out at his brother.

We installed tongue and groove flooring in the living room.

Many different tongues can be overheard in the dining hall of the United Nations.

Beth wanted to blurt out the secret, but she held her tongue.

Tennis shoes have wide tongues.

Tongue twisters are fun to try.

BODY

Using a new shampoo gave her hair lots of body.

Doug works at a body shop in Tennessee.

Michelle works at the Body Shop in the mall.

She has a great body.

Dr. Miranda has an extensive body of knowledge of medieval texts.

Lake Superior is a large body of water.

HEART

The Renaissance Center is in the heart of downtown Detroit, MI.

The heart transplant operation lasted seven hours.

Sylvia's last place finish in the triathlon showed she had a lot of heart.

I won't tell a soul, cross my heart.

Luigi put capers, black olives and artichoke hearts in the spaghetti sauce.

ARM

Julia ran into Lyle's arms when she met him at the airport.

Smith and Wesson is a small arms manufacturer.

The client's enthusiasm was a shot in the arm for the ad campaign.

The knight's shield included his coat of arms.

The legislative arm of the United States government is made up of the House and Senate.

I'd give my right arm for tickets to the concert!

LEG

Florence ran the last leg of the relay race.

The Robertsons generally have leg of lamb for Easter brunch.

One leg of the table was shorter than the others.

Ignore Fred and George; they are just pulling your leg!

The attorney knew his client didn't have a leg to stand on in his defense.

Beginning equestrians generally need a leg up to mount their horses.

The airline didn't serve any food on the last leg of my trip.

MOUTH

The mouth of the river is in Wisconsin.

We stood in the mouth of a cave.

The pharmacist said to take the medicine by mouth.

The bratty boy would always mouth off to the teacher.

Jamal was feeling pretty down in the mouth.

Invitation to the party was by word of mouth.

Karen performed mouth-to-mouth resuscitation on the stricken man.

HEAD

Dave likes a big head on his beer.

To make a salad, start with a head of lettuce.

Well, Eric, you have hit the nail on the head.

Tex lost 30 head of cattle to coyotes last year.

Rowdy Yates hollered, "Head 'em out!"

Natasha, go to the head of the line.

Group Three: Meanings in Action

DRAW

Sally likes to draw pictures of cats.

The dodgeball game ended in a draw.

The women would draw water from the well in the morning.

The cowboy beat the bad guy to the draw.

Horses were used to draw plows.

The magician asked an audience member to draw a card.

Cleo liked drawing attention to herself.

The student nurse had to learn how to draw blood.

DRIVE

It takes Jayson 20 minutes to drive to work.

Ofelia lives at 863 Maple Drive.

Our company sponsors a blood drive every three months.

Owen just didn't have the drive to start his own business.

You drive me nuts!

Anika's drive went from the tee right into the sand trap.

SIGN

Kate is learning to sign.

Please sign the permission slip for the field trip.

A dove is a sign of peace.

Campaign signs were posted all over town.

The sign said to take the next exit for the zoo.

TALK

Sylvia talks fast.

The police officer gave a safety talk at the assembly.

After hours of interrogation, the spy finally talked.

Jamie and her mom had a serious talk about Jamie's poor grades.

There's talk of our company downsizing after the merger.

Don't talk back to your mother!

When I call my sister, she talks my ear off!

WALK

It's a long walk to the library.

Marta planted tulips all along the walk.

Trainers walk the horses after a race.

Tigers walk through tall savannah grasses.

Carlos raised $200 in the Walk for Hope.

Don't talk the talk if you can't walk the walk.

CARRY

We practiced the fireman's carry.

After the championship game, the crowd got carried away.

Jeanette carried the twins to term.

The television station carried the election results.

The candidate carried 22 states.

Beverly's voice carries across the room.

The store carries 23 different kinds of dog food.

TOUCH

I was touched by the number of cards and flowers I received after my operation.

The surgeon said it had been touch and go for a while.

After high school, I stayed in touch with my best friend.

The guys played touch football on the beach.

Bob Ross did a little touch-up on the painting.

My grandma just got a touch-tone phone.

MEASURE

Measure For Measure was written by Shakespeare.

A measure of flour was given to each refugee.

Measure twice, cut once.

In the third measure of the sonata, be sure to come in on the second beat.

The Senate enacted a new measure to control wildlife management areas.

Randy didn't measure up to Layla's father's expectations.

For good measure, he lectured them on the importance of financial security.

Group Four: Learning to Crawl Meanings

BABY

Nadia named her baby after her grandmother.

Don't be such a baby!

For dinner we had steak, mashed potatoes and baby carrots.

Lyn has five sisters; she's the baby of the family.

The Baby Boomer vote will have an effect on the election.

Greg bought a baby grand piano.

Oh, baby, I love you.

BALL

Throw me the ball!

Cinderella wore a blue dress to the ball.

We had a ball at the silent lunch.

Ouch! I got a tack stuck in the ball of my foot!

The umpire called ball four, so the batter took first base.

MILK

Jamie likes to drink chocolate milk.

Farmer John milks the cows twice a day.

Keiko milked the sad situation for all it was worth.

The Ghost of Christmas Present showed Scrooge the milk of human kindness.

The CEO went to prison for milking the investment fund.

STORY

Sara's apartment was on the fifth story.

Hessie's grandma did not give her that cookie; she's telling a big, fat story.

We watched *The Story of the Edmund Fitzgerald* on TV last night.

There was a story in today's paper about interest rates.

No matter how many times he was questioned, Henry stuck to his story.

CHAIR

None of the dining room chairs matched.

Gina made a rocking chair for her Nana.

Elizabeth was named the finance committee chair.

Katy played third chair clarinet in band.

LAP

Sit on my lap, and I'll read you a story.

Mr. Whiskers likes to lap milk from a saucer.

Estelle swam 100 laps every day.

After winning the lottery, Earl lived in the lap of luxury.

We sat on the beach and watched as the waves lapped against the shore.

DRUM

Jeff played the drum in band.

The rain drummed against the window.

Numan drummed his fingers on the table as he thought.

My heart was beating like a drum.

Mrs. Rodriguez drummed the times tables into the fifth graders' heads.

Jonathan was drummed out of the Marine Corps on a bad conduct charge.

DOG

Jesse was dog-tired at the end of the marathon.

Mom dogged me to finish my homework.

Madeline returned my book to me all dog-eared.

Sometimes it is best to just let sleeping dogs lie.

Susie is cute, but Liz is a dog.

CAT

Siegfried and Roy work with big cats.

My dad drives the Cat on the construction site.

Josh didn't study much in college; he preferred to cat around.

The police caught the cat burglar.

Group Five: A Meanings Wardrobe

BELT

Ed wore a brown belt with black pants.

Troy qualified for his green belt in karate.

The mechanic changed my oil, the air filter and replaced the fan belt.

Civic leaders are looking for ways to revive cities in the Rust Belt.

Complaining to my supervisor instead of coming to me was below the belt.

Bill was glad to have his first solo flight under his belt.

He makes me so mad I just want to belt him in the mouth!

COAT

Christine got a new winter coat.

Give the ceiling another coat of paint in an hour.

The bridge was coated with ice.

The guinea pig's coat was soft.

Coat the banana in chocolate, roll it in nuts, and freeze.

Tiffany applied another coat of nail polish.

DRESS

Cindy got a new dress for the first day of school.

The school adopted a dress code.

Inez and Sophie love to play dress up.

The dress rehearsal for *The Fantasticks* lasted three hours.

My aunt always makes the dressing for the Thanksgiving turkey.

Daryl got a real dressing down from the coach for missing practice.

SLIP

Your slip is showing.

To return an item to the store, you need the sales slip.

Be careful not to slip on the ice.

Our profits began to slip in July.

For a good table, slip the maitre d' $50.

The boat slip cost $600 a year.

I meant to pay the bill, but it slipped my mind.

TIE

Railroad ties are made of wood.

I bought daddy a tie for Father's Day.

I can tie a half-hitch knot.

The hockey game ended in a tie.

I can't meet with you today; I'm tied up.

Louann took lessons on how to tie flies for fishing.

Lisa and Nick tied the knot on Valentine's Day.

PANTS

Boys outgrow their pants so quickly!

Sally can't wait; she has ants in her pants!

Jack's dog pants after a good run.

The Cubs beat the pants off the Cardinals.

HAMPER

Test anxiety hampered my progress in college.

Throw your dirty clothes in the hamper.

The picnic hamper was filled with sandwiches, chips and sodas.

The dancers' movements were hampered by their costumes.

CAP

Mikey got a cap gun for his birthday.

The rigger ran to cap an oil gusher.

Representative Carter pledged to create a tax cap.

Carlos put on his cap and gown for commencement.

Everyone knew Betty had set her cap for Richard.

When Lonny returned my car, the gas cap was missing.

PURSE

Lauren's new purse cost $26 on eBay.

After Dad got laid off, the whole family had to tighten the purse strings.

Emily pursed her lips in thought.

The purse for the heavyweight championship is the largest in boxing history.

CROWN

The king's crown was made of gold.

Brian got a gold crown on his tooth.

Winning the pageant was Lupe's crowning moment.

Larry ordered a Crown Royal on the rocks.

Group Six: Meanings Take Shape

SHORT

First graders are short.

A mouse's legs are short.

This ribbon is too short to go around the package.

The basketball coach gave a short talk at the pep rally.

Scooter bought three pairs of shorts for her vacation in Orlando, FL.

Martin Short was a regular on *Saturday Night Live*.

Terry ordered the short stack at the restaurant.

Kobe wanted to go to the game, but he was short on funds.

SQUARE

A square has four 90-degree angles.

The job came with a bunk and three square meals a day.

The concert was held in the town square.

If you are a square, you are probably not very popular.

Square dancing is popular at county fairs.

The crowd circled around as Joe and George squared off to fight.

SPLIT

Cheerleaders must be able to do splits.

Casey ordered a banana split.

When the cops showed up at the party, we split.

Bonnie and Clyde split the money from the hold-up.

Natalie and Jeremy split up for a while but got back together again.

After a day at the office, Kaela came home with a splitting headache.

ROUND

Give these volunteers a big round of applause!

Some people still believe the earth is flat, not round.

A round of cheese, fruit and crackers make great appetizers.

"Row, row, row your boat" is a round.

Lincoln loved to ride the merry-go-round at the park.

LONG

I long for my mom's meatloaf.

The play was four hours long.

Sonny caught a trout that was 10 inches long.

Winning the lottery is long shot.

The word "place" has a long "a" sound.

My brother has a long memory; he remembers every little thing I did to him growing up.

The hotel charges extra for long distance calls.

FRONT

I'll meet you in front of the Olive Garden.

The candy store was a front for gambling.

Sid will front you the money to start your business for a share of stock.

Karl has to sit in front of the classroom to hear the teacher.

Walk in front of me.

A cold front moved across the Midwest.

Bob Hope often entertained troops at the front.

BACK

My back hurts.

Back me up on this, OK?

Wait, let me back up and start over.

Josh backed the car into a shrub.

The start-up company was looking for a financial backer.

Jerry draped his jacket on the back of the chair.

There was a ruckus in the back of the theatre.

CENTER

Bob played center on the basketball team.

They often studied together at the student center.

When I bite into a bonbon, I hope the center is caramel.

Shelley and Rosina spent hours together at the shopping center.

The courthouse is in the center of the town.

Zsa Zsa is self-centered.

Group Seven: Meanings With Class

SPELL

Children learn to spell in school.

The wizard cast a spell on the village.

The contract will spell out the duties of each party.

Hazel and Helen often sat a spell on the porch rockers.

TABLE

We bought a new dining room table.

Mrs. Nelson drummed the times tables into the fifth graders' heads.

We will table all new business until we have a quorum.

Table C reflects a significant increase in students studying abroad.

The manager paid the staff under the table.

Pete could drink anyone under the table.

Set the table please.

ROOM

The room would only hold 40 people.

The candidate worked the room for votes.

There wasn't room in the hot tub for Dennis.

My job at the national park included room and board.

Sasha's evaluation indicated there was room for improvement.

I love ordering room service when I stay at the Hilton.

CLASS

Clare has no class, no class at all.

Jane Eyre, in the novel by Charlotte Bronte, married above her class.

There's a really high-class restaurant downtown that only seats eight people.

The third-grade class went on a field trip to the museum.

SCHOOL

While we were scuba diving, we swam through a giant school of fish.

Parents in the 1960s followed Benjamin Spock's school of thought on raising children.

Alexi began to school her horse.

Sharon attended Central Elementary School.

Carroll got his education at the school of hard knocks.

BOOK

The police arrested and booked the man on three felony counts.

The victims of the crime wanted the judge to throw the book at him.

Delores was able to book a table at Sardi's on Friday night.

The latest book by Maeve Binchey is a on the best-seller list.

After school was out, we'd book to the beach.

READ

The interviewer couldn't get a good read on the applicant.

My bill was high, so I asked the electric company to send out someone to read the meter.

As the police officer placed the suspect in handcuffs, he began to read him his rights.

The doctor monitored the patient's readout from the EEG machine.

ART

Teaching is an art.

I studied art history before going to Rome.

"Our Father, Which Art in Heaven…"

I graduated from the college of arts and sciences.

Art is cleaning out the basement.

PRACTICE

Mona would practice the violin three hours a day.

It is a good practice to look both ways before crossing the street.

Robyn has her own veterinary practice.

Track practice is every day after school.

I can't juggle four balls anymore, I'm out of practice.

Mark is a practicing ovo-lacto vegetarian.

FLAG

We begin the day by saluting the flag.

Donald asked the doorman to flag a taxi for him.

Flag that file for immediate review.

When the professor droned on and on, the students' interest began to flag.

Group Eight: Meanings in Place

HOUSE

The museum houses more than 1,200 works of art.

There was a large house for the opening of the new musical.

Buying a new house is exciting.

All legislation must originate in the house.

The next round of drinks is on the house.

TRAIN

Darn! I lost my train of thought.

Managers hate to train new employees.

The train to Versailles left on time.

The wedding gown had a long lace train.

CAMP

My family likes to camp in the woods.

Mr. Johnson switched to my opponent's camp.

The cult movie was pure camp.

Hundreds of thousands died in German concentration camps.

TEMPLE

Jan's migraines usually started at her left temple.

Rachel's bat mitzvah was held in the temple.

The excavation revealed the temple of Artemis.

My mom tried to curl my hair just like Shirley Temple's.

PARTY

Randy had his birthday party at the skating rink.

A rescue party was assembled when the plane crashed.

Lynn invited her friends to a Tupperware party.

The party of the first part cedes ownership of the boat to the party of the second part.

McCarthy sought out members of the Communist Party in the 1950s.

The hostess seated a party of four in a booth.

STORE

Squirrels store nuts for the winter.

John just ran out to the store.

Kaisha has a surprise in store for her!

The computer can store 60 MGHz of memory.

Flour stores well in a cool, dry place.

HOME

Mom always made our house a home.

Make yourself at home.

The Cubs played two games at home and three away.

The pitcher or the catcher can cover home, if the batter hits a pop-up.

He drove his point home with graphics.

STAGE

Ellen felt her destiny was the stage.

Ben took the last stage out of town to Denver, CO.

The plan required three stages.

The protestors staged a three-day sit-in.

The stage collapsed under the performers.

CLUB

Deanne and Elmer play cards at the deaf club every Saturday.

On the last hand, Elmer called clubs trump.

Terry ordered a club sandwich for lunch.

Tom got a new golf club for his birthday.

Claire likes to drink club soda with a lime twist.

The policeman used his club to subdue the rioters.

COURT

The trial goes to court in February.

Opal lives on Sycamore Court.

Andre built a private tennis court.

Jacques Bernaisonne was part of King Louis XIV's court.

Does anyone court their sweetheart anymore?

Building houses along flood plains is courting disaster.

Group Nine: A Feast of Meanings

TOAST
Will likes peanut butter toast.

The best man offered a toast to the bride and groom.

After losing the top account, Anthony was toast at the ad agency.

After an afternoon of skiing, it feels good to toast your feet at the fireplace.

Toast a marshmallow for s'mores.

SANDWICH
Cucumber and watercress sandwiches were served for tea.

My son's specialty is a grilled cheese sandwich.

The tour group was sandwiched into the tram headed for the top of the mountain.

The trip to the top of the mountain was sandwiched between the tours of the museum and the aquarium.

The file was sandwiched in between stacks of papers in the "IN" box.

CHICKEN
The kids were playing chicken with their hot rods on the back roads.

Malik didn't want to jump off the high dive because he was chicken.

Don't count your chickens before they hatch!

Earl put up a chicken wire fence.

I don't know why I stay at this job because I work for practically chicken feed.

BREAD
I need to make some bread fast, to pay the bills.

We had the whole family to break bread together at Thanksgiving.

I wouldn't take the job because it would have taken the bread out of the other guy's mouth.

Selling widgets was the company's bread and butter.

Bread sang *Baby I'm-a Want You* in the 1970s.

EGG

Honestly, Jimmy was naughty enough without Tim egging him on!

When the marketing plan flopped, Ted had egg on his face.

Theresa ate a hard-boiled egg.

The boys decided to egg Mr. Thorwald's house.

Thad is a good egg.

BUTTER

Butter the teacher up, so she won't give us a test.

I butter my toast before I eat my eggs.

I like to use butter and apple butter.

She's a real butterfingers.

Jasmine acts sweet, but butter wouldn't melt in her mouth.

WATER

Be sure to water the plants while I'm gone.

The smell of the steaks on the barbeque made my mouth water.

Kevin is in hot water now!

Janet's water broke on the way to the hospital.

Vivian bought a bottle of lavender toilet water.

The accusations of theft didn't hold water.

At the wedding reception, the champagne flowed like water.

POP

We bought bologna, bread and pop for lunch.

Dennis decided to pop the question to Connie.

Let's pop in and see Rose and Eddie!

Kimberly knew she shouldn't pop the zit on her nose.

The goal of the game was to pop your balloon.

Pop the cork, and let's get this party started!

We used to pop corn over the campfire.

My pop can lick your pop!

LICK

My dad can lick your dad!

The farmer put out a salt lick for the deer.

Young man, if you don't stop right now, I'll give you a licking!

The vet knew the dog was going to be OK when it licked her face.

Don't lick your lips when they're chapped.

Group Ten: A Cabinet of Meanings

SALT

Edith has to monitor her salt intake.

A sailor's language is often salty.

I take campaign speeches with a grain of salt.

The miser had a fortune salted away.

Olivia has been so helpful; she's the salt of the earth.

CAN

Merle got canned at work yesterday.

Patsy would always can peaches in the summer.

During half-time, I go to the can.

Can that noise! I'm not telling you again!

He can play chess, but he's not really good at it.

Take this garbage out to the trash can, please.

BOX

Quentin learned to box at the gym.

I have a box at the post office.

Lily mailed a box at the post office.

We sat in the jury box.

He stepped into the batter's box.

Alaine boxed the glassware before the movers came.

The Phantom sits in box 41 at the theatre.

PLATE

Rhonda brought a vegetable plate to the potluck.

The museum fund-raiser dinner was $100 a plate.

The umpire brushed off home plate.

Denise set the table with dinner, salad and bread plates.

The ushers passed the offering plate around the congregation.

The artist prepared the plates for the limited run prints.

Kelly was stressed because she had too much on her plate.

GLASS

Enrique had a glass jaw and was knocked out in the first round of the boxing match.

Wanda bought different colored glasses for each of the kids at Burger King.

The sculpture was made of glass.

The lake was as smooth as glass.

As Associate Director, Martha had reached the glass ceiling at her company.

FORK

The salad fork is smaller than the dinner fork.

The meat fork is there in the utensil drawer.

Murphy used a pitchfork to clean out the stables.

Fork over the money you owe me.

Yogi Berra said, "When you come to a fork in the road, take it!"

SPOON

The lovers spooned each other in bed.

Viola and Ned were spoonin' on the porch swing.

Evelyn carefully spooned soup into her elderly father's mouth.

John Robert caught a prize-winning bass on a spoon.

People say that George was born with a silver spoon in his mouth.

Group Eleven: Descriptive Meanings

SOLE

Joyce did not burn the soles of her feet walking across the hot coals.

Interpreting is my sole means of support.

Filet of sole is a delicious main course.

The soles of Horatio's shoes were worn to a nub.

TIGHT

The girls in the dance recital wore multicolored tights.

After downing a fifth of vodka, Stan was tight.

As friends go, Michelle and Debi are tight.

My girdle is too tight!

The school district operated under a tight budget.

It was a tight race to the finish line, but LaVondra won.

STEEP

Let the tea steep for a few minutes.

It's a steep trail down the Grand Canyon.

Tuition at Harvard is pretty steep!

THIN

The bridge was covered with a thin sheet of ice.

Larry's hair is thinning.

The clerk looked at me with a thin smile but did give me a refund.

Tom knew he was skating on thin ice in his relationship with Marcia.

Slice the ham for the sandwiches thin.

The orthopedic surgeon used a thin wire to hold the bone in place.

The air is thin as you ascend Mt. Everest.

Gladys went out to the garden to thin out the weeds.

The crowd thins out after Sammy Sosa's last at-bat of the game.

SMART

The scrape on her knee smarted.

Her outfit is smart.

The students are smart.

Louis is a smart aleck.

Smart Money says invest in health technology stocks.

FINE

The library fine came to $26.35.

Mary has very fine hair.

The Blue Moon serves very fine wines.

There is a fine line between love and hate.

Oh, baby, you are lookin' fine!

BROKE

An epidemic of a new strain of flu broke out.

She broke out in hives.

Charlie broke the bank in Las Vegas, NV.

After going on a wild spending spree, he was broke.

The suspect broke down after hours of questioning and admitted his guilt.

The microwave broke.

The game broke out into a bench-clearing brawl.

A blood vessel broke in Tara's arm.

The storm broke after raging for three hours.

Deidre's heart broke when Sean broke up with her.

She broke into tears at the break of dawn.

Her voice broke as she answered the phone.

When he declared his love for her after all, a smile broke across her face, and she broke into song.

Mark Spitz's record for the most gold medals won in a single Olympics stood for 36 years before Michael Phelps broke it in 2008.

LIGHT

The sack of groceries was light to carry.

Karen painted the kitchen a light yellow.

As it was his first offense, the judge gave a light punishment.

Rick bummed a cigarette off me then asked for a light.

Tanya felt lightheaded after drinking a Long Island Iced Tea.

Group Twelve: Public Service Meanings

JUDGE

It's hard to judge distance in the fog.

The judge ruled on the defense attorney's objection.

Gerald is a good judge of character.

Judge Reinhold appeared in the *Beverly Hills Cop* movies.

Andy will judge the pickle entries at the county fair.

NURSE

Rick studied to become a nurse.

La Leche League supports women who choose to nurse their babies.

After surgery, it is important to nurse the incision so it doesn't become infected.

Miss Haversham nursed her disappointment and anger for years.

Whenever we all went out to Lucky's, TC would nurse one beer all night long.

ORDER

PFC Pyle followed the sergeant's orders.

The vending machine is out of order.

Bummy ruled the motion was out of order.

I placed an order for several DVDs online.

In order to win the prize, you have to sell the most cookies.

Please arrange these files in alphabetical order.

Greg worked for three years as a short-order cook.

POLICE

The police arrested the escaped felon.

The Police sang *Every Breath You Take*.

Volunteers policed the park after the company picnic.

LOCK

Jack bought a lock for his bicycle.

Be sure to lock the door when you go out.

Jayson is a lock for MVP.

The ship made its way through the locks at Sault Sainte Marie.

Haley put a lock of her daughter's hair in her baby book.

The two deer's antlers got locked together as they fought.

The manager bought my sales pitch lock, stock and barrel.

Group Thirteen: Meaning Odds and Ends

ODD

Elijah has always been a little bit odd.

Place all files that end in an odd number in the red basket.

Walter Matthau and Jack Lemmon starred in *The Odd Couple*.

There were 60-odd people at the party.

Ray earned extra money by doing odd jobs.

Why is there always an odd sock in every load of laundry?

FIRE

The house is on fire!

The new manager will fire up to 300 employees.

Fire the pot in the kiln.

Ryan has too many irons in the fire.

The mascot and the cheerleaders worked to fire-up the fans.

Before you fire your pistol, make sure the range is clear.

SMOKE

Dennis started to smoke when he was 15.

He would borrow a smoke from his brother every day after school.

The pan on the stove began to smoke.

The smoke filled the room.

All summer long, DJ would smoke the fish he caught in the lake.

The police came up with a scheme to smoke out the thief.

Where there's smoke, there's fire.

MELT

The snow will melt in March.

Pete ordered a patty melt and a side of onion rings.

Aunt Carolyn's apple pie just melts in your mouth.

The Wicked Witch melted after Dorothy threw water on her.

When I looked into Fernando's brown eyes, I could feel myself melt.

Butter wouldn't melt in her mouth.

END

The movie was so boring I didn't think it would ever end.

I'd like an end piece of the roast, please.

Team Canada won the first end in the curling match.

Kerry was going to see the process through to the bitter end.

You need to honor your end of the bargain.

Melissa caused no end of trouble when she visited us.

Group Fourteen: A Potpourri of Meanings

SCORE

The opera score called for more than 100 voices.

Scores of people gather to watch the swallows return to Capistrano.

The score was tied after two quarters.

You should score steak before cooking it.

I have a score to settle with you!

Randy scored the winning touchdown.

FLOAT

Violet ordered a root beer float.

Frank had to replace the toilet float.

Yasmine learned to float on her back in swim class.

The wreckage of the ship floated on the water.

Could you float me a loan until payday?

The junior class float won the prize at the homecoming parade.

QUARTER

Meet me at the library at a quarter past ten.

We split the cheesecake into quarters.

I've collected all the newly minted state quarters.

The army will provide your food, clothing and sleeping quarters.

The Vikings surged ahead in the third quarter of the Super Bowl.

BOUND

The hostage was securely bound.

He was put in a car bound for the hideout.

He was bound and determined to escape.

The kidnappers were bound to make a mistake.

David's kick sent the ball out of bounds.

The St. Bernard bounded toward me.

TAG

Most kids love to play tag.

The pitcher tagged out the runner at first base.

The shirt tag gave cleaning instructions.

My crummy sister had to tag along on my dates.

CABLE

Send a cable to congratulate the winners.

Connect the black cable to the television.

You can get up to 136 different channels if you have cable.

Dean played Lt. Cable in the community theatre production of *South Pacific*.

CHECKER

Gramps plays checkers in the park.

He had a checkered past.

The highlight was taking the checkered flag at the Indy 500.

For a short time, he drove a checker cab in New York City, NY.

He spent most of his life, though, as a supermarket checker.

DIRT

I got the dirt on the woman Trent has been seeing!

The children collected dirt samples for science class.

I got the living room furniture dirt cheap.

When I was growing up, we were dirt poor, let me tell you.

Incoming…hit the dirt!

SWELL

Sarah twisted her ankle playing basketball, and it began to swell.

Darrell sure is a swell guy.

Dirk really has a swelled head, doesn't he?

When Marnessa was handed her diploma, her mom just swelled with pride.

The boat began to toss as the swells broke against its side.

Group Fifteen: A Meanings Grab Bag

STIR

Stir the chocolate syrup into the milk.

Not a creature was stirring, not even a mouse.

Trevor is always looking to stir up some trouble.

The actress' backless gown caused quite a stir.

Big Louie spent 15 years in the stir.

WELL

"Well," said Tony, "I guess I'll see you tomorrow."

The women would draw water from the well early in the morning.

I hope your father-in-law gets well soon.

After some initial difficulties, business is now going well.

Sandy paid well over the value of the painting because she liked it.

Jim and Tanya are making ends meet, but they're not well off.

Leave well enough alone.

DATE

Marcus and Janine's first date was dinner and a movie.

Lew has a November 3 court date.

Please be sure to date the invoice.

On this date in history, the Americans with Disabilities Act was signed into law.

Kasha added figs and dates to the fruit plate.

Bell bottoms go in and out of date.

LAND

International flights often land in foreign lands.

I fell while roller skating and landed on my wrist and broke it.

The cat fell out of a third-story window and landed on its feet.

Caleb bought good land for planting wheat.

"My land!" exclaimed Granny Wright.

FREEZE

Give the water time to freeze.

Marcy thought she'd freeze to death at the football game.

"Freeze!" shouted the police officer.

My heart froze when I saw Danny wander into the road right in front of a car.

Until the bankruptcy hearing was over, the bank put a freeze on company assets.

The music video used a cool series of freeze-frame pictures of the singer.

I always freeze on essay tests.

When we go to the Tastee-Freeze, I get a chocolate dip-top cone.

FEED

The shelter depends on donations to feed approximately 150 people a day.

When Dorothy lived on the farm, it was her job to feed the chickens.

Harold pays me chicken feed for all the work that I do.

My Uncle Hersch has an extensive collection of feed caps.

The news team was waiting for the satellite feed of the breaking story.

Chrissa spent the day feeding quarters into the slot machine.

The church put on a good feed for the fundraiser.

Unit Two:

Variations on a Sign

Introduction

In American Sign Language (ASL), some signs have a contextual meaning which can be modified to show different uses, situations and applications. For example, the word "catch" in the exercise below means to receive a thrown object. How you show the process of "catching" the object depends upon several factors:

▶ What body part(s) you might use to do the receiving (fingertips, one or both hands, your arms, your body, your mouth, etc.)

▶ The size and shape of what was thrown

▶ The intensity with which the object was thrown

▶ The weight and durability/fragility of the object thrown

▶ Whether the object is being thrown up, down or across to a receiver

There are other considerations that impact the way the sign is made.

▶ Is the person who is catching:

• nervous?	• angry?
• skilled or clumsy?	• determined?
• ill?	• eager?
• older or younger?	• careless?

▶ Who is doing the throwing?

▶ What is her mood or attitude?

▶ What is the relationship between the one who does the throwing and the one who is catching?

• For example, a dating couple in the midst of a fight might throw and catch car keys differently than a surprised birthday girl getting keys for her first car from her father.

Consider modifications for the standard sign "catch" indicating catching the following objects below. Then create sign variations representing the different people and contexts where catching these objects might occur.

CATCH

a frisbee

a basketball

pizza dough

a baseball

a baby tossed in the air

a bride's bouquet

a beanbag

Mardi Gras beads

a note passed in study hall

a sandbag

a football

car keys

an egg-toss egg at a picnic

a medicine ball

a popcorn kernel

a baton

a tennis ball

hard candy

a stage diver in a mosh pit

a can of baked beans

Variation One: PUT ON

gloves	a ski mask
a scarf	a belt
a turtleneck	a bathrobe
a leotard	a coat
a cowboy hat	earrings
a necklace	a too-tight ring
a commencement cap and gown	a child's party hat
a tie	a wedding dress
a jockstrap	a cummerbund

Next, show how the signs above change based on the person putting on the various objects. Is the person older or younger? Hurried? Nervous? Sleepy?

What if the person has a broken arm?

How does each sign change if the person puts the various items on another person as compared to herself? A date? A child? A patient? A student?

How does each sign change if the nature of the item changes? (For example, clip-on earrings, pierced earrings with posts or wires, a long muffler for the cold as compared to a fashion accessory scarf? Wrapped? Tied? Knotted?)

Variation Two: DRINK

a shot of whiskey

from a water fountain

a frozen margarita

cough syrup

a can of pop

a to-go mocha

milk from a coconut

hot cocoa with marshmallows

from a flask

a milkshake

hot tea

from the garden hose

from a water bottle

a box of juice

an individual can of pineapple juice

communion wine

from a novelty hat that holds beer cans

from a milk jug

Next, show how the signs above change based on who is doing the drinking.

Is the person a toddler? A character in a movie? Sober? Sexy? Trying to make an impression? On a date? Driving?

How does the person hold each kind of container?

How does the person drink from each kind of container?

How does the temperature of the drink affect the way the person drinks?

What happens if the flow of the drink suddenly changes?

Is the cough syrup on a spoon, in a small cup or straight from the bottle?

Variation Three: OPEN

a window	a safe
an oven door	a greeting card
a bottle of champagne	a new CD
a book	a letter
a gag snake-in-a-can	a locker
a file drawer	a ring box
your cat's mouth	a cooked bag of microwave popcorn
a door of a haunted house	an aspirin bottle
a box of cereal	a heart-shaped locket

Next, show how the signs above change based on the person doing the opening.

Is the person nervous? Bored? Tense? Hopeful?

What if the person opening the various objects has arthritis?

What if the person is an amputee and uses a hook?

How does the person hold the object being opened? Is it easy or hard to open?

Does the locker open with a combination or a key? How does the sign for opening a combination locker differ from the sign for opening a safe?

What is the person's reaction after opening each item?

Variation Four: PAINT

the trim in the room   designs on a ceramic pot
an airplane model   a portrait
your name on an overpass   a wall
a picket fence   the Sistine Chapel Ceiling
fingernails   a T-shirt
a stencil on a wall   a child's face at a carnival

Next, show how the signs above change based on the person doing the painting.

Is the person attentive or sloppy? Professional or amateur?

What size and shape is the paint brush? How is the person holding it?

How big or small is the paint container? How is the person holding it?

How does the paint brush go in and out of its container?

Is there a lot or only a little paint in the container?

Is the paint fresh or old and dry?

How do you sign spray cans or squeeze bottles getting plugged up? How do you sign fixing this problem?

Variation Five: PICK

strawberries

a chocolate from a box

a lobster from the tank for your dinner

nits

a book off a shelf

an apple from a tree

burrs off a dog

petals off a daisy

a handful of flowers

your nose

a scab

roses

underwear that has ridden up/a wedgie

Next, show how the signs above change based on the person doing the picking.

How does a person pick when she doesn't want to be seen or noticed?

Is the picking for fun or work?

What if the item that's being picked is resistant?

How is picking nits different when it's your child's head as compared to when it's done by apes?

What if there's a potential for injury (e.g., a plant has thorns, a lobster has claws, a scab is not healed)?

Variation Six: BLOW

a balloon up	the petals off of a white dandelion
a bubblegum bubble	out a candle
out birthday candles on a cake	excess glitter off a craft project
a trumpet	soap bubbles
on a hot beverage to cool it	a harmonica
like the wolf in *The Three Little Pigs*	on your hands to warm them

Next, show how the signs above change based on the person doing the blowing.

Is the person younger or older?

Is the person doing the action willingly or because someone else wants him to?

What happens if the person blows too hard or too softly?

How does the person hold the object(s) being blown?

Variation Seven: BRUSH

hair	your teeth
a Lhasa Apso	a pony
a toilet	a cow for the state fair
lint off a suit	vegetables
your nails	shoes being shined

Next, show how the signs above change based on the person doing the brushing.

Is the person brushing her own hair? Someone else's hair? A child's? A client's? A doll's?
Is the hair long or short?
Is there fringe around a bald part?
Are there tangles?

Is the person brushing his own teeth or someone else's? A child's? A dog's? Dentures?

How does the person hold the different brushes?

How does the person interact with the thing being brushed? Does the person pat the cow/pony/dog with the other hand while brushing?

Is the person paid to clean the toilet or is it housework? Is the toilet in a home? A bus station? A fraternity?

Variation Eight: WASH

plates and bowls	the car
your unmentionables in the sink	a head of lettuce
silverware	hair
potatoes	the dog
glasses and cups	the cat
the table	your face
your child's face, with tissue and spit	the floor

Next, show how the signs above change based on the person doing the washing.

Does this person always get stuck doing this job?
Is he making the best of it? Enjoying it?

Is the person doing this at work or at home? How are those two tasks done differently?

What implement(s) are used? A cloth? A brush? A sponge?

How does the person hold the items(s) that are being washed? Does the person wear gloves?

How is washing a knife different from washing a spoon?

How is washing a water glass different from washing a champagne glass?

How is washing plates that were rinsed different from washing ones that sat with spaghetti sauce hardening on them?

How big or small is the sink or the tub?

From where are the items being picked up to be washed?

Where are the items placed after they are washed?

Variation Nine: WRAP

a large-framed print
a heavy book
a used piece of gum
a quilt
a can of nuts
myself in a blanket

a pair of socks
a bottle of wine
a pair of diamond stud earrings
a Scrabble game
a glass-blown unicorn
glasses in newspaper for packing

Next, show how the signs above change based on the person doing the wrapping.

Is the person skilled? Old or young?

Does the person enjoy doing this?

Is the gift to be wrapped being given with love? Obligation? One-upmanship?

Is the wrapping paper on a roll or folded in sheets?

Is the tape in a dispenser or only on a roll? Can the person find the end of the tape? Does she use the dispenser, scissors or teeth to cut it?

Is the person wrapping in a hurry?

How does the person have to hold the object as it's being wrapped?

Does the end result look pretty and neat or more like "it's the thought that counts?"

Variation Ten: EAT

soup	a banana
grapes	a pear
spaghetti	a spoonful of peanut butter
a corndog	beef jerky
watermelon	an ice cream cone
a Big Mac	crackers and cheese
popcorn	an unfamiliar food
potato chips	a taco
chicken	pizza
caramels	sunflower seeds

Next, show how the signs above change based on the person doing the eating.

Is the person engaging only in the activity of eating or doing another simultaneous activity (e.g., driving, reading, watching a movie)?

Is the person eating alone or with others? How would the person eat the item differently if he was alone as compared to eating in front of others?

How does the person eat with family at home as compared to in a restaurant or with the boss in a restaurant?

What eating utensil does the person need to eat this item? How does the person hold the utensil or item that is being eaten?

Is the popcorn in a bowl, a bucket or a bag? Does the person eat one kernel at a time or handfuls?
How does the person funnel a handful of popcorn into her/his mouth?

Is the pizza out of a box? On plates? Eaten with a fork? From the crust side or the point side?

Variation Eleven: ZIP

a coat	pants
a skirt	go-go boots
a leather motorcycle jacket	a pencil case
a backpack	a tent flap
a dress	a fanny pack
a sleeping bag	a purse

Next, show how the signs above change based on the person doing the zipping.

Are the person's hands steady or shaking?
Does the person doing the zipping do it slowly or quickly?

Is the person making a particular statement reflected in the zipping? Is the person zipping up or unzipping?

Is there more than one zipper that needs zipped?

Is the person zipping his own item or zipping for another person?

Is the zipper in the front, back or side?

Is the zipper long or short?

Is the zipper tab broken?

Variation Twelve: CARRY

a baby	a serving tray
a stack of books	a cup of coffee
several plastic bags of groceries	a box
two paper bags full of groceries	a basket
a load of firewood	a purse
a ring-bearer's pillow	a bag of potting soil
a slice of pizza	a pizza box
the Olympic torch	a bowl of soup
a mouse by the tail	a Ming vase
a baby bird	a suitcase

Next, show how the signs above change based on the person doing the carrying, as well as the size and shape of the object(s) being carried.

Is the object light or heavy?

Is the object big or small?

How does the sign change if the object is big and heavy as compared to big and light? Small and heavy as compared to small and light?

Can the person keep a grip on what's being carried? What happens when the person's grip starts to slip?

Is the object being carried in front of the body, on a hip, on the head, over the shoulder or on the back?

How does the sign change if the person doing the carrying is a child? An elder? A person who has limited use of his hands and arms?

What if the person is unhappy or unwilling to do the carrying?

Variation Thirteen: PULL

a book off a shelf	the bus-stop signal
a slot machine lever	a toy from a dog's mouth
a wagon	a hair out of your food
a child's tooth	a rabbit out of a hat
weeds	off a piece of dental floss
up an anchor	a ceiling fan chain
a cow's teat for milking	the starter on a chainsaw
a nose hair	a rolling suitcase

Next, show how the signs above change based on the person doing the pulling, as well as the object being pulled.

Is the person young or old? Has the person done this kind of pulling before or is this a new experience?

Is the book being pulled from a shelf thick or thin? Is it being pulled off a shelf that's eye-level, higher or lower?

What's in the wagon? Does it require both hands to pull? Is it easier to face forward or turn around and face the wagon while pulling? What happens if the person pulls uphill versus downhill?

Can the anchor be pulled up hand-over-hand or is it on a winch? How stable is the boat?

Is the dog big or small? Does the dog want to give up the toy? What shape is the dog's toy--round, a rope, a bone? Is there slobber on it?

What's the consistency of the food in which the hair is found? Does the hair come out of the food easily? Is the hair long or short?

Is the bus-stop signal within reach? Is the ceiling fan chain within reach? How many pulls on the chain are required to adjust the speed of the fan?

Is the cow cooperative? Who's doing the pulling--a farmer doing a demonstration or a volunteer? How confident or willing is the volunteer?

Variation Fourteen: POUR

cake batter into a pan
liquid into test tubes
cereal out of a box
tea from a teapot
lemonade from a pitcher
chocolate syrup into milk

water out of a shoe
Mr. Bubble into your bath
a can of pop into a glass
wine into a glass
gravy on mashed potatoes
water from a bucket

Next, show how the signs above change based on the person doing the pouring and what is being poured.

Are the person's hands steady or shaking?

How does the person hold the various containers?

Is this person pouring for herself or someone else?

How does the consistency of what's being poured change the manner of pouring?

What happens if the liquid comes out too fast or too slow?

What happens when the person is done pouring?

Variation Fifteen: TURN ON/OFF

the lights	a car
a microwave	an older model television
a calculator	a stove
a blender	a washing machine
a computer	a fire alarm
an outside water spigot	a lawn mower
a TTY	a cell phone

Next, show how the signs above change based on the person doing the action of turning something on or off, as well as the object that's being turned on or off.

Is there a switch, knob, handle or button?
Does the person need to flip the switch, turn the knob, push or pull the button?

Would a person use just one finger, a knuckle or a whole hand to operate the object?

Is there resistance in the mechanism or does it respond to a light touch? What if the mechanism is fairly worn out and doesn't respond right away?

What if a person isn't sure about how exactly to turn an object on or off?

How would a person make adjustments once the object is turned on: making the lights brighter or dimmer, the stove hotter or cooler or the water flow faster or slower from the spigot?

Unit Three:

One Sign, Many English Words

Introduction
Some words have a similar core meaning and comprise a group of English synonyms. Exactly which synonym is used in a conversation depends upon several factors, including:
- who is speaking
- the audience (one or more persons…or the dog, mirror reflection, pet rock, etc.)
- the setting or context
- the topic
- the mood (of both the speaker and audience)
- the relationship between the speaker and audience (e.g., peers, equal or unequal power/status/social class, level of education, new or long-time acquaintance)

Consider the word "beautiful." The dictionary defines it as "delighting the senses or mind" *[Webster's Encyclopedic Dictionary of the English Language, 1989]*. Many English words are used to convey the idea of "beautiful," such as attractive, good-looking, eye candy, glamorous, a knockout, a beaut, easy on the eyes, hot, gorgeous, a looker and lovely. Which word might a bride's grandmother murmur to the grandfather as the bride comes down the aisle? Which word might a used car salesman use to a customer interested in a car? Which word might a teenage boy use to describe the *Sports Illustrated* swimsuit edition cover girl to a pal? Which word might a polite friend use in describing a newborn to the baby's parents?

American Sign Language (ASL) expresses variations of meaning of the standard sign "beautiful" by modifying it with appropriate movement, facial expression and/or body language. Signs are executed with movements that are bigger, smaller, slower, faster or repeated to create a specific meaning. Facial expressions reflect the accompanying mood and affect of the speaker.

Practice creating variations of the sign "beautiful" by doing the following exercise:

1. With a partner or in a group, brainstorm as many English synonyms as you can for the word "beautiful."
2. Create a scenario by choosing options from the lists below; choose a speaker, audience, setting and mood.
3. Decide upon their social status in relationship to each other and how long they have known each other.
4. Imagine a conversation they would have in which they would be discussing something either (or both) of them finds beautiful.

5. Choose a synonym from your list that best reflects the word choices they would make within the conversation.
6. Decide how you would modify the sign "beautiful" to express each speaker's meaning.
7. Demonstrate how the sign would vary depending upon the speaker's mood.
8. Add other potential speakers, audiences, settings and moods to the lists to create additional scenarios.

Speaker	Audience	Setting	Mood
car salesman	friend	grocery store	bored
teenager	minister	reunion	desperate
truck driver	celebrity	wedding	awed
family member	grandma	airplane	proud
People magazine reporter	teenager	living room	hurried
waitress	baby	bowling alley	shy
photographer	cat	park	amused

Variation One: HAPPY

1. Brainstorm English synonyms for the sign "happy."
2. Create a scenario from the lists below by choosing a speaker, audience, setting and mood.
3. Decide upon the social status and length of the relationship between the speaker and audience.
4. Decide upon the conversational topic (what they're talking about).
5. Choose a synonym that would best fit their conversation.
6. Decide how you would modify the sign "happy" to express the speaker's exact meaning.
7. Demonstrate how the sign would vary depending upon the speaker's mood.
8. Add other speakers, audiences, settings and moods to the list to create additional scenarios.

Speaker	Audience	Setting	Mood
teacher	boyfriend	swimming pool	distracted
mechanic	buddy	baseball game	thoughtful
daycare worker	spouse	restaurant	nervous
lobbyist	travel agent	bedroom	determined
child	child	office	confident
job interviewer	parent	miniature golf course	egotistic

Variation Two: TO VOMIT

1. Brainstorm English synonyms for the sign "to vomit."
2. Create a scenario from the lists below by choosing a speaker, audience, setting and mood.
3. Decide upon the social status and length of the relationship between the speaker and audience.
4. Decide upon the conversational topic (what they're talking about).
5. Choose a synonym that would best fit their conversation.
6. Decide how you would modify the sign "to vomit" to express the speaker's exact meaning.
7. Demonstrate how the sign would vary depending upon the speaker's mood.
8. Add other speakers, audiences, settings and moods to the list to create additional scenarios.

Speaker	Audience	Setting	Mood
senior citizen	doctor	emergency room	calm
college student	parent	office	concerned
kid	buddy	lounge	frantic
paramedic	teacher	restaurant	impressed
person with an eating disorder	waitress	bus	exhausted
parent	coach	mall	disgusted

Variation Three: AFRAID

1. Brainstorm English synonyms for the sign "afraid."
2. Create a scenario from the lists below by choosing a speaker, audience, setting and mood.
3. Decide upon the social status and length of the relationship between the speaker and audience.
4. Decide upon the conversational topic (what they're talking about).
5. Choose a synonym that would best fit their conversation.
6. Decide how you would modify the sign "afraid" to express the speaker's exact meaning.
7. Demonstrate how the sign would vary depending upon the speaker's mood.
8. Add other speakers, audiences, settings and moods to the list to create additional scenarios.

Speaker	Audience	Setting	Mood
traveler	group	coffee shop	boastful
teenager	seatmate	class	introverted
hostage	friend	airplane	gentle
driving instructor	spouse	hospital	impatient
child	reporter	theatre lobby	brave
parent	psychiatrist	living room	bossy

Variation Four: TO KILL

1. Brainstorm English synonyms for the sign "to kill."
2. Create a scenario from the lists below by choosing a speaker, audience, setting and mood.
3. Decide upon the social status and length of the relationship between the speaker and audience.
4. Decide upon the conversational topic (what they're talking about).
5. Choose a synonym that would best fit their conversation.
6. Decide how you would modify the sign "to kill" to express the speaker's exact meaning.
7. Demonstrate how the sign would vary depending upon the speaker's mood.
8. Add other speakers, audiences, settings and moods to the list to create additional scenarios.

Speaker	Audience	Setting	Mood
termite specialist	ROTC members	rally	bold
hit man	neighbor	conference	sly
peace activist	policeman	office	sad
Navy SEAL	Army recruit	school	brave
reverend	son	arcade	wild
videogame player	congregation	street corner	distant
crime victim	teenager	porch	pitying

Variation Five: TO BE DRUNK

1. Brainstorm English synonyms for the sign "to be drunk."
2. Create a scenario from the lists below by choosing a speaker, audience, setting and mood.
3. Decide upon the social status and length of the relationship between the speaker and audience.
4. Decide upon the conversational topic (what they're talking about).
5. Choose a synonym that would best fit their conversation.
6. Decide how you would modify the sign "to be drunk" to express the speaker's exact meaning.
7. Demonstrate how the sign would vary depending upon the speaker's mood.
8. Add other speakers, audiences, settings and moods to the list to create additional scenarios.

Speaker	Audience	Setting	Mood
child	judge	office	remorse
college buddies	college buddies	bar	humorous
bartender	spouse	court room	cooperative
police officer	sibling	AA meeting	accusing
spouse	social worker	den	curious
social worker	truck driver	emergency room	resigned

Variation Six: MONEY

1. Brainstorm English synonyms for the sign "money."
2. Create a scenario from the lists below by choosing a speaker, audience, setting and mood.
3. Decide upon the social status and length of the relationship between the speaker and audience.
4. Decide upon the conversational topic (what they're talking about).
5. Choose a synonym that would best fit their conversation.
6. Decide how you would modify the sign "money" to express the speaker's exact meaning.
7. Demonstrate how the sign would vary depending upon the speaker's mood.
8. Add other speakers, audiences, settings and moods to the list to create additional scenarios.

Speaker	Audience	Setting	Mood
dealer	tourist	used car lot	stingy
thief	parent	crack house	excited
minister	women's group	casino	miserable
investor	loan officer	church	patient
teenager	landlord	bank	suspicious

Variation Seven: PREGNANT

1. Brainstorm English synonyms for the sign "pregnant."
2. Create a scenario from the lists below by choosing a speaker, audience, setting and mood.
3. Decide upon the social status and length of the relationship between the speaker and audience.
4. Decide upon the conversational topic (what they're talking about).
5. Choose a synonym that would best fit their conversation.
6. Decide how you would modify the sign "pregnant" to express the speaker's exact meaning.
7. Demonstrate how the sign would vary depending upon the speaker's mood.
8. Add other speakers, audiences, settings and moods to the list to create additional scenarios.

Speaker	Audience	Setting	Mood
teenager	husband	court	worried
doctor	girlfriend	restaurant	secretive
girlfriend	boyfriend	bathroom	joyful
wife	judge	office	betrayed
social worker	child	on the telephone	overwhelmed

Variation Eight: ANGRY

1. Brainstorm English synonyms for the sign "angry."
2. Create a scenario from the lists below by choosing a speaker, audience, setting and mood.
3. Decide upon the social status and length of the relationship between the speaker and audience.
4. Decide upon the conversational topic (what they're talking about).
5. Choose a synonym that would best fit their conversation.
6. Decide how you would modify the sign "angry" to express the speaker's exact meaning.
7. Demonstrate how the sign would vary depending upon the speaker's mood.
8. Add other speakers, audiences, settings and moods to the list to create additional scenarios.

Speaker	Audience	Setting	Mood
parent	supervisor	jail	quiet
boss	clerk	living room	assertive
grandparent	partner	office	sneering
prostitute	police officer	fast food restaurant	puzzled
teenager	teenager	store	intense

Variation Nine: TO CRY

1. Brainstorm English synonyms for the sign "to cry."
2. Create a scenario from the lists below by choosing a speaker, audience, setting and mood.
3. Decide upon the social status and length of the relationship between the speaker and audience.
4. Decide upon the conversational topic (what they're talking about).
5. Choose a synonym that would best fit their conversation.
6. Decide how you would modify the sign "to cry" to express the speaker's exact meaning.
7. Demonstrate how the sign would vary depending upon the speaker's mood.
8. Add other speakers, audiences, settings and moods to the list to create additional scenarios.

Speaker	Audience	Setting	Mood
child	parent	therapist's office	restrained
sibling	teacher	gym	drained
caretaker	friend	movie theatre	unsure
lawyer	workout partner	church	surprised
soldier	counselor	living room	manipulative

Variation Ten: TO DIE

1. Brainstorm English synonyms for the sign "to die."
2. Create a scenario from the lists below by choosing a speaker, audience, setting and mood.
3. Decide upon the social status and length of the relationship between the speaker and audience.
4. Decide upon the conversational topic (what they're talking about).
5. Choose a synonym that would best fit their conversation.
6. Decide how you would modify the sign "to die" to express the speaker's exact meaning.
7. Demonstrate how the sign would vary depending upon the speaker's mood.
8. Add other speakers, audiences, settings and moods to the list to create additional scenarios.

Speaker	Audience	Setting	Mood
movie director	students	office	shocked
pathologist	relative	assembly	delighted
counselor	Marine	classroom	cautious
veterinarian	detective	dining room	grieving
parent	toddler	field trip	vengeful

Variation Eleven: TO POOP

1. Brainstorm English synonyms for the sign "to poop."
2. Create a scenario from the lists below by choosing a speaker, audience, setting and mood.
3. Decide upon the social status and length of the relationship between the speaker and audience.
4. Decide upon the conversational topic (what they're talking about).
5. Choose a synonym that would best fit their conversation.
6. Decide how you would modify the sign "to poop" to express the speaker's exact meaning.
7. Demonstrate how the sign would vary depending upon the speaker's mood.
8. Add other speakers, audiences, settings and moods to the list to create additional scenarios.

Speaker	Audience	Setting	Mood
patient	group of friends	cruise ship	ill
nurse	nurse	store	relieved
college student	3 year old	attended care facility	exasperated
tourist	patient	break room	revolted
babysitter	doctor	mall	embarrassed

Variation Twelve: LIE

1. Brainstorm English synonyms for the sign "lie."
2. Create a scenario from the lists below by choosing a speaker, audience, setting and mood.
3. Decide upon the social status and length of the relationship between the speaker and audience.
4. Decide upon the conversational topic (what they're talking about).
5. Choose a synonym that would best fit their conversation.
6. Decide how you would modify the sign "lie" to express the speaker's exact meaning.
7. Demonstrate how the sign would vary depending upon the speaker's mood.
8. Add other speakers, audiences, settings and moods to the list to create additional scenarios.

Speaker	Audience	Setting	Mood
youth	teacher	a date	being nice
policeman	banker	in a classroom	nervous
CEO	teenager	at an interview	totally serious
best friend	parole officer	in a restaurant	forceful
married man	repairman	on the telephone	smooth
addict	news reporter	at a bar	guilty

Variation Thirteen: TIRED

1. Brainstorm English synonyms for the sign "tired."
2. Create a scenario from the lists below by choosing a speaker, audience, setting and mood.
3. Decide upon the social status and length of the relationship between the speaker and audience.
4. Decide upon the conversational topic (what they're talking about).
5. Choose a synonym that would best fit their conversation.
6. Decide how you would modify the sign "tired" to express the speaker's exact meaning.
7. Demonstrate how the sign would vary depending upon the speaker's mood.
8. Add other speakers, audiences, settings and moods to the list to create additional scenarios.

Speaker	Audience	Setting	Mood
patient	doctor	office	ambivalent
therapist	spouse	bedroom	grumpy
college student	friend	mall	desperate
spouse	colleague	bar	stressed
ambulance driver	toddler	elevator	matter-of-fact

Variation Fourteen: FIRED

1. Brainstorm English synonyms for the sign "fired."
2. Create a scenario from the lists below by choosing a speaker, audience, setting and mood.
3. Decide upon the social status and length of the relationship between the speaker and audience.
4. Decide upon the conversational topic (what they're talking about).
5. Choose a synonym that would best fit their conversation.
6. Decide how you would modify the sign "fired" to express the speaker's exact meaning.
7. Demonstrate how the sign would vary depending upon the speaker's mood.
8. Add other speakers, audiences, settings and moods to the list to create additional scenarios

Speaker	Audience	Setting	Mood
football coach	group of employees	staff meeting	disbelieving
manager	employee	bus	worried
buddy	spouse	loading dock	relieved
spouse	roommate	restaurant	angry
public relations rep	local & national media	auditorium	nervous
63 year old	parents	break room	consoling

Variation Fifteen: FOOD

1. Brainstorm English synonyms for the sign "food."
2. Create a scenario from the lists below by choosing a speaker, audience, setting and mood.
3. Decide upon the social status and length of the relationship between the speaker and audience.
4. Decide upon the conversational topic (what they're talking about).
5. Choose a synonym that would best fit their conversation.
6. Decide how you would modify the sign "food" to express the speaker's exact meaning.
7. Demonstrate how the sign would vary depending upon the speaker's mood.
8. Add other speakers, audiences, settings and moods to the list to create additional scenarios.

Speaker	Audience	Setting	Mood
teenaged boy	dieters	kitchen	bored
anthropologist	friends	skate park	ravenous
Army private	chefs	auditorium	hopeful
dietician	school assembly	parking lot	hopeless
actor	siblings	food pantry	enthused
nanny	homeless person	barn	impatient
farmer	helpers/assistants	cafe	frustrated
survival expert	waitress	cafeteria	delighted

Unit Four:

What Does It Mean?

Introduction

There are certain words and phrases in English that would not make sense if you signed them word-for-word in American Sign Language (ASL). These figurative words and phrases have more complex meanings than the surface words imply. Several signs may be needed to convey the meaning. In order to create more precise equivalent meanings, think about a dictionary definition or ways to explain the meaning to a person who had never before encountered the words or phrases. Elements of the ASL sign-string might include:

- a definition or explanation
- a description of what it looks like
- a list of items that describe the category
- a comparison to what it is not

Consider the phrase "blind date." ASL does have a sign for "blind" in the sense that one does not have the sense of sight. ASL also has a sign for "date" meaning an event when, typically, two unmarried people come together for a social meeting. But those two signs together do not express the meaning of the phrase. A "blind date" does have elements of the ASL sign for "date." However, the participants themselves are not necessarily blind. Rather, they are people who haven't met before and have been matched up by family, friends, the Internet or a dating agency. A "blind date," then, is a particular kind of date. Using the sign for "date," then explaining the circumstances that define that date, would be a way of conveying the meaning of the phrase.

In the next exercises, don't be concerned that a translation takes time or uses a lot of explanation at this point. The initial goal is to create understanding, not speed. With practice, the ability to identify key elements that efficiently and concisely convey meaning will develop.

With a partner or in a group, discuss the meaning of the following words and phrases. After you have determined the meaning of the phrase, decide how you would convey that meaning in ASL.

Group One
Party pooper
Toll-free number
To be in the doghouse
Cry wolf

Group Two
Field trip
Over-the-counter drugs
First things first
Keep up with the Joneses

Group Three
Eye chart
Make-up test
Walk on eggshells
Let the cat out of the bag

Group Four
Police line-up
Nickname
Keep it under your hat
Skeleton in the closet

Group Five
Warts and all
Splitting hairs
Tighten your belt
Coast-to-coast

Group Six
Puppy love
Feel out of place
Not my cup of tea
Cream of the crop

Group Seven
Traffic jam
As clear as mud
To make a long story short
No ifs, ands or buts about it

Group Eight
Off-color joke
Fanny pack
To have dibs
No strings attached

Group Nine
The fine print
The more, the merrier
Money burning a hole in your pocket
Six of one, a half dozen of the other

Group Ten
Submarine sandwich
Have a sweet tooth
Food for thought
Leave a bad taste in your mouth

Group Eleven

Computer virus

Keynote speaker

That's the last straw

Every Tom, Dick and Harry

Group Twelve

In a pickle

Junk food

Fruit cup

In one ear and out the other

Group Thirteen

Blood is thicker than water

Easier said than done

Reality show

Drag queen

Group Fourteen

Penny pincher

Money talks

It never rains, but it pours

Speak of the devil

Group Fifteen

It takes all kinds

Key ring

Family tree

Pyramid scheme

For Further Reading

Larson, M. L. (1998). *Meaning-based translation: A guide to cross-language equivalence.* Lanham, MD: University Press of America.

Massoud, M. M. F. (1988). *Translate to communicate: A guide for translators.* Elgin, IL: David C. Cook Foundation.